vjbnf

921 HOOVER

S0-BAO-132

Rumsch, BreAnn 1981- author
Herbert Hoover
33410017167109   06-30-2021

★ THE ★
UNITED
STATES
PRESIDENTS

HERBERT
HOOVER

BreAnn Rumsch

**Checkerboard
Library**

An Imprint of Abdo Publishing
abdobooks.com

ABDOBOOKS.COM

Published by Abdo Publishing, a division of ABDO, PO Box 398166, Minneapolis, Minnesota 55439. Copyright © 2021 by Abdo Consulting Group, Inc. International copyrights reserved in all countries. No part of this book may be reproduced in any form without written permission from the publisher. Checkerboard Library™ is a trademark and logo of Abdo Publishing.

Printed in the United States of America, North Mankato, Minnesota
052020
092020

THIS BOOK CONTAINS
RECYCLED MATERIALS

Design: Emily O'Malley, Kelly Doudna, Mighty Media, Inc.
Production: Mighty Media, Inc.
Editor: Liz Salzmann

Cover Photograph: Library of Congress
Interior Photographs: Albert de Bruijn/iStockphoto, p. 37; AP Images, pp. 5, 6 (Hoover as student), 7, 13, 14, 19, 24, 36; Getty Images, pp. 23, 31, 32; Library of Congress, pp. 6, 7 (Lou Hoover), 16, 17, 20, 27, 40; MPI/Library of Congress, p. 29; National Archives, p. 18; National Park Service, pp. 6 (birthplace), 7 (graves), 11, 33; Pete Souza/Flickr, p. 44; Shutterstock Images, pp. 38, 39; Underwood & Underwood/Getty Images, p. 21; Wikimedia Commons, pp. 40 (George Washington), 42

Library of Congress Control Number: 2019956440

Publisher's Cataloging-in-Publication Data
Names: Rumsch, BreAnn, author.
Title: Herbert Hoover / by BreAnn Rumsch
Description: Minneapolis, Minnesota : Abdo Publishing, 2021 | Series: The United States presidents | Includes online resources and index.
Identifiers: ISBN 9781532193569 (lib. bdg.) | ISBN 9781098212209 (ebook)
Subjects: LCSH: Hoover, Herbert, 1874-1964--Juvenile literature. | Presidents--Biography--Juvenile literature. | Presidents--United States--History--Juvenile literature. | Legislators--United States--Biography--Juvenile literature. | Politics and government--Biography--Juvenile literature.
Classification: DDC 973.916092--dc23

★ CONTENTS ★

Herbert Hoover

Herbert Hoover was different from other politicians. Unlike other presidents, he was not a lawyer or even a great speaker. Instead, Hoover was a scientist and a businessman. He became a politician because he wanted to help others.

Hoover's parents died when he was young. So, an uncle raised him in Oregon. Hoover then went to college and became a successful mining **engineer**. During **World War I**, he led relief efforts in Europe. Then, Hoover worked as the US food **administrator** and the **secretary of commerce**.

In 1928, Hoover was elected the thirty-first US president. When he took office, the nation's **economy** seemed strong. But in late 1929, it started to fail. A long period of hardship fell across America. This time became known as the Great Depression. Many Americans blamed Hoover for their troubles.

Still, Hoover continued to work hard for America. In time, he was recognized for his great contributions to the United States and the world.

Herbert Hoover

★ TIMELINE ★

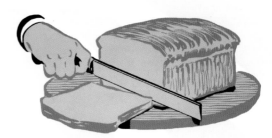

1874

On August 10, Herbert Clark Hoover was born in West Branch, Iowa.

1899

On February 10, Hoover married Lou Henry in California.

1900

In China, the Hoovers were caught in the Boxer Rebellion.

1917

President Woodrow Wilson appointed Hoover US food administrator.

1885

Hoover moved to Newberg, Oregon, to live with his uncle.

1895

Hoover graduated from California's Stanford University, where he studied geology.

1914

World War I began. Hoover headed the Commission for Relief in Belgium.

1908

Hoover began his own engineering company in London, England.

1919

Hoover directed the American Relief Administration.

1921

Hoover became secretary of commerce under President Warren G. Harding.

1932

Hoover established the Reconstruction Finance Corporation. He lost reelection to Franklin D. Roosevelt.

1944

Lou Hoover died on January 7.

1947 and 1953

Hoover served as chairman for the Hoover Commissions.

1929

On March 4, Hoover became the thirty-first president of the United States. The stock market crashed in October.

1939

World War II began. Hoover led the Polish Relief Commission.

1946

Hoover directed the Famine Emergency Committee.

1964

On October 20, Herbert Hoover died in New York City, New York.

" The imperative need of this nation at all times is the **leadership of Uncommon Men or Women.**"

DID YOU KNOW?

★ Hoover Dam is named in honor of President Hoover. It lies across the Colorado River on the border between Arizona and Nevada. Construction on the dam began in 1930 and it was finished in 1936. Today, it is the highest concrete arch dam in the United States.

★ Hoover was one of three presidents to give away his presidential salary. He gave his salary to charities. In addition, the Hoovers paid for social events at the White House with their own money.

★ In 1931, President Hoover signed an act that made "The Star-Spangled Banner" the national anthem.

★ Hoover loved the outdoors. He especially enjoyed fishing. He even wrote a book about this favorite hobby called *Fishing for Fun*.

Young Bert

Herbert Clark Hoover was born in West Branch, Iowa, on August 10, 1874. Everyone called him Bert. Bert's parents were Jesse and Hulda Hoover. Jesse worked as a blacksmith and sold farm machinery. Bert had a brother, Theodore, and a sister, May.

Bert and his family were **Quakers**. They believed in living a simple life, working hard, and helping others. These values stayed with Bert his whole life.

When Bert was six years old, his father died. Hulda held the family together. She worked as a **seamstress** and a Quaker minister. Sadly, Hulda died when Bert was nine. So relatives took in the Hoover children.

In 1885, Bert moved to Newberg, Oregon. There, he attended a Quaker school called Friends Pacific Academy. Bert lived with his uncle Henry John Minthorn, who was a doctor.

FAST FACTS

BORN: August 10, 1874

WIFE: Lou Henry (1874–1944)

CHILDREN: 2

POLITICAL PARTY: Republican

AGE AT INAUGURATION: 54

YEARS SERVED: 1929–1933

VICE PRESIDENT: Charles Curtis

DIED: October 20, 1964, age 90

Bert's birthplace in West Branch, Iowa

Three years later, Bert and his uncle moved to Salem, Oregon. In Salem, Minthorn started a **real estate** business. Bert worked there as an office clerk. At night, he took business classes.

Eventually, Bert decided to become an **engineer**. So in 1891, he moved to California. There, he attended a new school called Stanford University.

Student and Engineer

At Stanford, Hoover studied geology. He also managed a laundry business, delivered newspapers, and worked for the university. Hoover spent his summers working as an assistant geologist for the US government.

During his last year at Stanford, Hoover met Lou Henry. She was a fellow geology student. Hoover and Lou had much in common. They quickly fell in love.

In 1895, Hoover graduated from Stanford. Then, he took a job in a California gold mine. He pushed a mining car and shoveled ore. Hoover worked long hours and made little money. However, he gained valuable experience.

Hoover took a job with mining **engineer** Louis Janin in 1896. At first, Janin hired Hoover to work only as a typist. But he soon sent Hoover on mining jobs in New Mexico, Colorado, and Arizona.

In 1897, Janin helped Hoover get a job with Bewick, Moreing & Company of London, England. The company sent Hoover to Australia. There, he taught Australians about US mining methods. Hoover also managed a gold mine. It earned him and the company a lot of money.

At Stanford, Hoover (*lower left*) belonged to a student engineering group. Members of the group practiced surveying, or measuring land.

World Traveler

In 1898, Bewick, Moreing & Company offered Hoover a job in China. Hoover accepted. In a telegram, he proposed marriage to Lou. They were married in California on February 10, 1899. The next day, they boarded a ship to China.

The Hoover family. Seated are Hoover and his wife, Lou, who holds their granddaughter Peggy Ann. Their son Herbert Jr. (*right*) stands with his wife, Margaret, and his brother, Allan (*left*).

In China, Hoover acted as the chief **engineer** for the Chinese Imperial Bureau of Mines. He helped the Chinese government find many coal fields and minerals.

The Hoovers were caught in the **Boxer Rebellion** in 1900. They lived in a settlement in Tientsin with other foreigners. For almost a month, the settlement was under attack. During that time, Hoover supervised the construction of defenses. He also handed out food and water. Eventually, foreign troops arrived in China to stop the rebellion. The Hoovers had outlasted the danger.

The following year, Hoover became a partner with Bewick, Moreing & Company. On August 4, 1903, the Hoovers welcomed their first son, Herbert Jr. Five weeks later, the family set out on a world journey. Hoover looked for new business for the company. Then on July 17, 1907, the Hoovers had a second son, Allan.

By 1908, the Hoovers had settled in London, England. Hoover was now a wealthy man. He left Bewick, Moreing & Company and formed his own engineering company. He started mining projects and helped other companies manage their money.

Public Service

Hoover's new business was a success. However, he became bored with simply making money. Hoover wanted to move into public service. He found an opportunity to do this in 1914.

Posters from the US Food Administration encouraged Americans to observe "Meatless Mondays" and "Wheatless Wednesdays."

That year, **World War I** began in Europe. At the time, Hoover was still living in London. The war trapped thousands of Americans in Europe. Hoover organized a relief committee to help Americans get home safely.

Later that year, a British **blockade** stopped food shipments to Belgium. To help, Hoover headed the Commission for Relief in Belgium. It raised money to feed more than 9 million hungry Belgians. Hoover also formed other relief efforts during **World War I**. He helped feed and clothe millions of children affected by the war.

In 1917, America entered the war. President Woodrow Wilson called Hoover home and made him the US food **administrator**. The United States needed to have enough food to send to its troops fighting in Europe. So, Hoover asked Americans to not waste food and limit how much they ate.

After World War I ended, many people around the world were left homeless

About 14 million US families followed Hoover's food conservation program.

and hungry. Hoover directed the American Relief Administration in 1919. It fed 300 million people from 21 countries in Europe and the Middle East.

Secretary of Commerce

The Boulder Canyon Project Act of 1928 authorized the construction of what later became Hoover Dam.

Hoover's efforts in Europe made him famous. Many Americans thought he would make a good president. He decided to seek the **Republican** nomination for president in 1920.

However, the Republicans chose Warren G. Harding instead. Harding became the next president. Vice President Calvin Coolidge became president when Harding died three years later. Hoover became the **secretary of commerce**

President Coolidge (*left*)
and Secretary Hoover

in 1921. He kept the job for almost eight years. Hoover worked under presidents Harding and Coolidge.

As **secretary of commerce**, Hoover accomplished much. He wrote a highway safety code and improved airline safety. Hoover also encouraged industries to standardize their products. This lowered the cost of goods and created new jobs.

In 1921, Hoover planned irrigation and power developments along the Colorado River. His ideas eventually led to the construction of Hoover Dam.

In 1923, Secretary Hoover established and became president of the American Child Health Association. This organization improved hospitals and helped sick children in need.

Hoover also served as president of Better Homes in America throughout the 1920s. This organization lowered

As part of the Better Homes in America campaign, Hoover helped break ground at the construction site for a model home.

the cost of new homes. So, more Americans were able to become homeowners.

Then in 1927, the Mississippi River flooded. More than 600,000 people were affected by the disaster. Hoover quickly organized a flood relief program. It fed, clothed, and housed many thousands of flood victims.

Curtis (*left*) and Hoover campaigned together in 1928.

Hoover's great works continued to make him popular with Americans. In 1928, the **Republican** Party nominated Hoover to run for president. Senator Charles Curtis was nominated for vice president.

The **Democrats** nominated Alfred E. Smith. His **running mate** was Senator Joseph T. Robinson. In the election, voters made Hoover the thirty-first president of the United States.

President Hoover

Hoover took office on March 4, 1929. At the time, the United States was experiencing a period of great prosperity. President Hoover wanted every American to share in the nation's wealth. He hoped to see a nation "built of homeowners and farm owners."

To help Americans, President Hoover created many new organizations. The Federal Farm Board aided struggling farmers. The Veterans **Administration** cared for former members of the armed forces. And, the Federal Bureau of Prisons reformed US prisons.

In addition, Hoover pushed Congress to create a Department of Education. He proposed tax cuts for the poor. Hoover also reorganized the Bureau of Indian Affairs. This allowed it to better protect the rights of Native Americans.

The president did not stop there. He proposed a series of dams in Tennessee and California. Hoover established more national parks and monuments. He also enlarged many national forests. These projects created many new jobs.

To aid farmers, Hoover signed the Farm Relief Bill in 1929.

Meanwhile, people had been making money in the
stock market. However, many had borrowed money to
buy stocks they could not afford. Hoover knew this was

The stock market crash on October 24, 1929,
was the worst financial upset in US history.
The day became known as Black Thursday.

dangerous for the **economy**. So, President Hoover asked Congress for tougher banking laws.

But Congress ignored Hoover's requests. The banks kept lending money. More Americans went into **debt**. Then in October 1929, disaster struck the US **stock market**.

Stock prices crashed. People who had borrowed money to buy stocks could not repay their loans. Banks began to suffer. Even worse, many people lost their savings. People had less money to spend, so production slowed and businesses suffered.

A **recession** began. President Hoover tried to stop it. He asked business leaders not to fire people or cut their wages. He also asked state leaders to create jobs through **public works**.

But Hoover's plans did not work. The economy continued to slow. By 1931, nearly six million Americans were out of work. Those who held jobs had their wages cut. Banks began to shut down. The recession turned into the Great Depression. And the economy continued to worsen.

SUPREME COURT APPOINTMENTS

CHARLES EVANS HUGHES: 1930

OWEN ROBERTS: 1930

BENJAMIN NATHAN CARDOZO: 1932

PRESIDENT HOOVER'S CABINET

ONE TERM
March 4, 1929–March 4, 1933

- ★ **STATE:** Henry L. Stimson
- ★ **TREASURY:** Andrew W. Mellon
  Ogden L. Mills (from February 13, 1932)
- ★ **WAR:** James W. Good
- ★ **INTERIOR:** Ray Lyman Wilbur
- ★ **AGRICULTURE:** Arthur M. Hyde
- ★ **COMMERCE:** Robert P. Lamont
  Roy D. Chapin (from December 14, 1932)
  Patrick J. Hurley (from December 9, 1929)
- ★ **NAVY:** Charles Francis Adams
- ★ **ATTORNEY GENERAL:** William D. Mitchell
- ★ **LABOR:** James J. Davis
  William N. Doak (from December 9, 1930)

Hoover (*seated, center*) with his cabinet

The Great Depression

President Hoover believed America should help itself out of the Great Depression. But he also saw that his plans were failing. So, in January 1932, Hoover asked Congress to establish the Reconstruction Finance Corporation (RFC).

The RFC gave government money to large businesses and banks. Hoover hoped the RFC would help these businesses run smoothly again. Then they could give people jobs.

Hoover also asked Congress to approve **public works**. More than 800 public buildings and about 37,000 miles (60,000 km) of highway were built. These projects created many jobs.

Still, families across the nation were homeless. People everywhere waited in long lines for bread. Others marched through Washington, DC, to demand government relief.

In 1932, Hoover was up for reelection. He ran against New York governor Franklin D. Roosevelt. Roosevelt's **running mate** was **Speaker of the House** John N. Garner. The campaign was difficult. Many Americans blamed Hoover for the Great Depression. Roosevelt easily won the election.

Hoover's last days as president were challenging. In February 1933, banks across the country shut down. Hoover tried to turn the **economy** around. However, he did not have time to fix the nation's problems. The Great Depression would not end until 1942.

All over the country, homeless people built shack communities. These were called Hoovervilles. Other homeless people slept under newspapers called Hoover blankets.

After the White House

After leaving the White House in March 1933, the Hoovers split their time between two homes. One was in Palo Alto, California. The other was an apartment in the Waldorf-Astoria Hotel in New York City, New York.

Hoover stayed busy. In 1936, he served as chairman of the Boys Club of America. With Hoover's help, 500 new clubs were started. They gave homeless boys a safe place to go.

In 1939, **World War II** began when Germany attacked Poland. Hoover led the Polish Relief Commission. The organization provided food for thousands of Polish children during the war.

Then on January 7, 1944, Lou Hoover suffered a heart attack and died. Hoover missed his wife very much.

World War II ended in 1945. It had destroyed cities and caused food shortages across Europe. President Harry S. Truman asked Hoover to lead the Famine Emergency Committee. In 1946, Hoover directed the committee. It fed millions of Europeans while they rebuilt their cities and farms.

Hoover traveled to nearly 40 countries in 1946. While in Poland, he visited orphans. Hoover worked to find food for them and other victims of war.

In 1947 and 1953, Hoover served as chairman for two special government groups. They suggested ways to cut wasteful spending. The federal government took most of their suggestions. These groups later became known as the Hoover Commissions.

Hoover spent the rest of his days writing, giving speeches, and advising American presidents. By 1963, Hoover had grown ill. Yet he refused to give up his work. On October 20, 1964, Herbert Hoover died in New York City. He is buried near his childhood home in West Branch.

Though he was known as a great problem solver, Herbert Hoover faced a difficult presidency. Americans blamed him for the

Hoover's life after his presidency was active. In 1960, he still worked 8 to 12 hours per day.

Herbert and Lou Hoover are buried beside each other.
Their graves overlook Hoover's birthplace in West Branch.

Great Depression. But the problems that caused the depression were firmly in place when he took office. Not even Hoover's leadership skills could overcome them. Yet later in life, Hoover regained America's respect and praise for his hard work.

BRANCHES OF GOVERNMENT

The US government is divided into three branches. They are the executive, legislative, and judicial branches. This division is called a separation of powers. Each branch has some power over the others. This is called a system of checks and balances.

★ EXECUTIVE BRANCH

The executive branch enforces laws. It is made up of the president, the vice president, and the president's cabinet. The president represents the United States around the world. He or she oversees relations with other countries and signs treaties. The president signs bills into law and appoints officials and federal judges. He or she also leads the military and manages government workers.

★ LEGISLATIVE BRANCH

The legislative branch makes laws, maintains the military, and regulates trade. It also has the power to declare war. This branch consists of the Senate and the House of Representatives. Together, these two houses make up Congress. Each state has two senators. A state's population determines the number of representatives it has.

★ JUDICIAL BRANCH

The judicial branch interprets laws. It consists of district courts, courts of appeals, and the Supreme Court. District courts try cases. If a person disagrees with a trial's outcome, he or she may appeal. If a court of appeals supports the ruling, a person may appeal to the Supreme Court. The Supreme Court also makes sure that laws follow the US Constitution.

★ QUALIFICATIONS FOR OFFICE

To be president, a person must meet three requirements. A candidate must be at least 35 years old and a natural-born US citizen. He or she must also have lived in the United States for at least 14 years.

★ ELECTORAL COLLEGE

The US presidential election is an indirect election. Voters from each state choose electors to represent them in the Electoral College. The number of electors from each state is based on the state's population. Each elector has one electoral vote. Electors are pledged to cast their vote for the candidate who receives the highest number of popular votes in their state. A candidate must receive the majority of Electoral College votes to win.

★ TERM OF OFFICE

Each president may be elected to two four-year terms. Sometimes, a president may only be elected once. This happens if he or she served more than two years of the previous president's term.

The presidential election is held on the Tuesday after the first Monday in November. The president is sworn in on January 20 of the following year. At that time, he or she takes the oath of office:

> *I do solemnly swear (or affirm) that I will faithfully execute the office of President of the United States, and will to the best of my ability, preserve, protect and defend the Constitution of the United States.*

LINE OF SUCCESSION

The Presidential Succession Act of 1947 defines who becomes president if the president cannot serve. The vice president is first in the line of succession. Next are the Speaker of the House and the President Pro Tempore of the Senate. If none of these individuals is able to serve, the office falls to the president's cabinet members. They would take office in the order in which each department was created:

Secretary of State

Secretary of the Treasury

Secretary of Defense

Attorney General

Secretary of the Interior

Secretary of Agriculture

Secretary of Commerce

Secretary of Labor

Secretary of Health and Human Services

Secretary of Housing and Urban Development

Secretary of Transportation

Secretary of Energy

Secretary of Education

Secretary of Veterans Affairs

Secretary of Homeland Security

While in office, the president receives a salary of $400,000 each year. He or she lives in the White House and has 24-hour Secret Service protection.

The president may travel on a Boeing 747 jet called Air Force One. The airplane can accommodate 76 passengers. It has kitchens, a dining room, sleeping areas, and a conference room. It also has fully equipped offices with the latest communications systems. Air Force One can fly halfway around the world before needing to refuel. It can even refuel in flight!

Air Force One

If the president wishes to travel by car, he or she uses Cadillac One. It has been modified with heavy armor and communications systems. The president takes

Cadillac One

Cadillac One along when visiting other countries if secure transportation will be needed.

The president also travels on a helicopter called Marine One. Like the presidential car, Marine One accompanies the president when traveling abroad if necessary.

Sometimes, the president needs to get away and relax with family and friends. Camp David is the official presidential retreat. It is located in the cool, wooded mountains of Maryland. The US Navy maintains the retreat, and the US Marine Corps keeps it secure. The camp offers swimming, tennis, golf, and hiking.

When the president leaves office, he or she receives lifetime Secret Service protection. He or she also receives a yearly pension of $207,800 and funding for office space, supplies, and staff.

Marine One

George Washington

Abraham Lincoln

Theodore Roosevelt

	PRESIDENT	PARTY	TOOK OFFICE
1	George Washington	None	April 30, 1789
2	John Adams	Federalist	March 4, 1797
3	Thomas Jefferson	Democratic-Republican	March 4, 1801
4	James Madison	Democratic-Republican	March 4, 1809
5	James Monroe	Democratic-Republican	March 4, 1817
6	John Quincy Adams	Democratic-Republican	March 4, 1825
7	Andrew Jackson	Democrat	March 4, 1829
8	Martin Van Buren	Democrat	March 4, 1837
9	William H. Harrison	Whig	March 4, 1841
10	John Tyler	Whig	April 6, 1841
11	James K. Polk	Democrat	March 4, 1845
12	Zachary Taylor	Whig	March 5, 1849
13	Millard Fillmore	Whig	July 10, 1850
14	Franklin Pierce	Democrat	March 4, 1853
15	James Buchanan	Democrat	March 4, 1857
16	Abraham Lincoln	Republican	March 4, 1861
17	Andrew Johnson	Democrat	April 15, 1865
18	Ulysses S. Grant	Republican	March 4, 1869
19	Rutherford B. Hayes	Republican	March 3, 1877

LEFT OFFICE	TERMS SERVED	VICE PRESIDENT
March 4, 1797	Two	John Adams
March 4, 1801	One	Thomas Jefferson
March 4, 1809	Two	Aaron Burr, George Clinton
March 4, 1817	Two	George Clinton, Elbridge Gerry
March 4, 1825	Two	Daniel D. Tompkins
March 4, 1829	One	John C. Calhoun
March 4, 1837	Two	John C. Calhoun, Martin Van Buren
March 4, 1841	One	Richard M. Johnson
April 4, 1841	Died During First Term	John Tyler
March 4, 1845	Completed Harrison's Term	Office Vacant
March 4, 1849	One	George M. Dallas
July 9, 1850	Died During First Term	Millard Fillmore
March 4, 1853	Completed Taylor's Term	Office Vacant
March 4, 1857	One	William R.D. King
March 4, 1861	One	John C. Breckinridge
April 15, 1865	Served One Term, Died During Second Term	Hannibal Hamlin, Andrew Johnson
March 4, 1869	Completed Lincoln's Second Term	Office Vacant
March 4, 1877	Two	Schuyler Colfax, Henry Wilson
March 4, 1881	One	William A. Wheeler

Franklin D. Roosevelt

John F. Kennedy

Ronald Reagan

	PRESIDENT	PARTY	TOOK OFFICE
20	James A. Garfield	Republican	March 4, 1881
21	Chester Arthur	Republican	September 20, 1881
22	Grover Cleveland	Democrat	March 4, 1885
23	Benjamin Harrison	Republican	March 4, 1889
24	Grover Cleveland	Democrat	March 4, 1893
25	William McKinley	Republican	March 4, 1897
26	Theodore Roosevelt	Republican	September 14, 1901
27	William Taft	Republican	March 4, 1909
28	Woodrow Wilson	Democrat	March 4, 1913
29	Warren G. Harding	Republican	March 4, 1921
30	Calvin Coolidge	Republican	August 3, 1923
31	Herbert Hoover	Republican	March 4, 1929
32	Franklin D. Roosevelt	Democrat	March 4, 1933
33	Harry S. Truman	Democrat	April 12, 1945
34	Dwight D. Eisenhower	Republican	January 20, 1953
35	John F. Kennedy	Democrat	January 20, 1961

★ ★ ★

LEFT OFFICE	TERMS SERVED	VICE PRESIDENT
September 19, 1881	Died During First Term	Chester Arthur
March 4, 1885	Completed Garfield's Term	Office Vacant
March 4, 1889	One	Thomas A. Hendricks
March 4, 1893	One	Levi P. Morton
March 4, 1897	One	Adlai E. Stevenson
September 14, 1901	Served One Term, Died During Second Term	Garret A. Hobart, Theodore Roosevelt
March 4, 1909	Completed McKinley's Second Term, Served One Term	Office Vacant, Charles Fairbanks
March 4, 1913	One	James S. Sherman
March 4, 1921	Two	Thomas R. Marshall
August 2, 1923	Died During First Term	Calvin Coolidge
March 4, 1929	Completed Harding's Term, Served One Term	Office Vacant, Charles Dawes
March 4, 1933	One	Charles Curtis
April 12, 1945	Served Three Terms, Died During Fourth Term	John Nance Garner, Henry A. Wallace, Harry S. Truman
January 20, 1953	Completed Roosevelt's Fourth Term, Served One Term	Office Vacant, Alben Barkley
January 20, 1961	Two	Richard Nixon
November 22, 1963	Died During First Term	Lyndon B. Johnson

	PRESIDENT	PARTY	TOOK OFFICE
36	Lyndon B. Johnson	Democrat	November 22, 1963
37	Richard Nixon	Republican	January 20, 1969
38	Gerald Ford	Republican	August 9, 1974
39	Jimmy Carter	Democrat	January 20, 1977
40	Ronald Reagan	Republican	January 20, 1981
41	George H.W. Bush	Republican	January 20, 1989
42	Bill Clinton	Democrat	January 20, 1993
43	George W. Bush	Republican	January 20, 2001
44	Barack Obama	Democrat	January 20, 2009
45	Donald Trump	Republican	January 20, 2017

Barack Obama

★ PRESIDENTS MATH GAME ★

Have fun with this presidents math game! First, study the list above and memorize each president's name and number. Then, use math to figure out which president completes each equation below.

1. Richard Nixon – Herbert Hoover = ?

2. Herbert Hoover + Thomas Jefferson = ?

3. Herbert Hoover – Abraham Lincoln = ?

Answers: 1. John Quincy Adams (37 – 31 = 6)
2. Dwight D. Eisenhower (31 + 3 = 34)
3. James Buchanan (31 – 16 = 15)